CONTENTS

ACKNOWLEDGMENTS

Grateful thanks to all who helped and supported me with this book: Anna, Jane, David, Michael, my fellow traveller Jenny, and to my cosmic dancers at home - Rupert, Damien and Alex.

FOREWORD
by Sir George Trevelyan

Julie Soskin has channelled this statement from a high spiritual source, which urges us to face and accept drastic earth changes with courage and joy, knowing that Planet Earth is to be cleansed and a new epoch begun.

This book is for all who have grasped the reality of the spirit realms and can see that we are privileged to take part in the cleansing of the planet in the coming years. It is so grand a picture that it puts our individual troubles and problems into true perspective. I urge you to read it and grasp that you have incarnated to take part in this momentous change. The Beings on the higher plane call on us to go forward with courage and joy, knowing that "death" is the great illusion.

Julie has done a fine deed in giving us this book. It is like a clarion call for spiritual activity as we approach the new millennium.

INTRODUCTION

The man at the bottom of the mountain sees a very different view from the one at the top, or even the one in between. All swear they are right. I will not swear, but will endeavour to describe my view.

Up until three years ago, I connected to spirit as a medium with total submission, and was completely happy to do so. I had been taught that way and it felt right. One day, with very little warning, I had an experience which I cannot describe in words but the result was a change in awareness and it was because of this change that I asked my good friend and colleague Jenny Grant to help me find some answers. We asked to be connected to the highest source of light available to us. It described itself as "a synthesis of energy, Original Thought". After six sessions of being given personal information, we were told that a book would be dictated. "The Wind of Change" was that book. The ease with which it became published was my confirmation that it was right. When the manuscript was handed over to the publishers, I abdicated responsibility - it never was a part of me anyway. This incidentally is why it is difficult to answer questions on the text. However, I do try and would like to thank all the people who have written to me with their good wishes.

My work as a medium continues, but the usual evidence of survival rarely comes. With most sitters, what have been described as the hierarchy guides come through with spiritually based information. They will not allow us to lean on them, and indeed my information is that they are the last astral link before the connection to the Source. This connection can only be made by the individual who unfolds the many layers covering their soul light, and as a teacher I endeavour to open doors for students to contact this light. When connection is made, there is automatic access to the "main computer", so to speak! All the answers are within: now is the time to listen to your own truth.

As that energy becomes stable and grows, there is a point of connection of consciousness whereby all other souls of similar vibration automatically link. This is the point where man ceases to *think* he wants to help - he just does.

It is my greatest joy to see the power of the human spirit at work, and the soul awakening, pulling us into realisation. We are also seeing the perceptions of man, opening us up to accommodate the different dimensions. There will always be those who cannot see, but in every walk of life there are more who can. Once the soul has been touched, even if only for a moment, the progress of that individual is assured.

Wishing you all great joy.

JULIE SOSKIN.

ODE TO THE EARTH

Oh you green Earth, you vibrant soul,
You alone have held the key to lies and truth;
You alone have freed the captive heart within
your globe,
You alone have been the school of knowledge,
With its special laws and circumstances.

We have watched and learned much from your
pain,
We tell you now it is coming to a close;
The trumpets ring out, heralding the new
beginnings,
The forces of want and desire are fleeing your
pleasant lands.

But oh, dear children of the green planet Earth,
You never did appreciate the realms of experience
At your touch, the smell, the sights and sound,
Your perfectly balanced Earth, the green light of
love
In the universe.

But sing the song of freedom now, it is time to
move on!
A new sun will climb on your horizon -
A sun of pure white light;
And as the poles meet, all colours, all experiences
Will finally be a conscious unison of the whole.

I. OPPORTUNITY

We come again, dear children of light, in this time of turbulent change. We have spoken before of energies and magnetism; we will continue with this theme, endeavouring to explain that which is transpiring now.

Some aspects of this information are impossible for your minds to grasp, so at various points we will give you analogies and paint a mental picture. This will be somewhat inadequate, but is the best that we can do in order for you to understand. The pictures we paint will act as springboards, stimulating and promoting your higher intuitions.

There is an energy field around your globe, a tangible field which cannot be seen, but can be found. There is also an energy that radiates from your bodies, an energy that emanates from all living things on Earth. The energy of your planet shifts and changes. There are forks of energy, power lines. These are Earth's vibrant forces.

Many of your instruments are powered by electricity. These instruments have different functions, and yet the energy which powers them is the same. So it is with everything in the Cosmos. All and everything emanates from the Source. Animals, plants, planets and stones, all from the same beginning, from the same release of the cosmic breath.

The energy of the Earth radiates from deep within, moving outwards in lightning-like veins. Because of the structure of your Earth, these veins are in constant flow. These are your power lines. Some of them are very symmetrical, some of them are straight. Long ago, at a time when you did not wear shoes on your feet, these energy fields had a tremendous effect upon you. There were places of energy that people recognised as "good places" and "bad places". Men, in those days, were intuitively aware of these power veins, and as a consequence worked with this, planting their crops and living in certain areas. They did not know about energy, but they sensed these emanations of power. Now, so much has been covered over, your senses are numbed, but these energies can still be felt.

These energies have nothing to do with the people who lived in a place, or what transpired there. They are to do with the Earth's energy. Now, all this is being rediscovered. Both intuitively and scientifically, all is coming to light. And because of the greater intelligence of man and the expansion of man's knowledge, his perception will be very different from that of people in bygone years, who sensed these energies but knew not what they were. Science will acknowledge intuition. Much will be spoken of energies. This will be a word much in use.

You will not worship energies. You will not create sacred places as man did in the past. You will understand them to be an integral part of your living, breathing planet, and eventually you will be able to use them as power sources. Because when the energy from the sun mixes through an enhancer with the energy of the Earth, you have access to enormous power. This power would not have been used wisely by recent generations, indeed it would have been used unwisely. But now you are nearing the time when you can use this knowledge with intelligence and discrimination, for the good of the whole. And once you are able to harness this source of energy, which is so cheap, so clean and simple, starvation will not be possible. We have intentionally spoken often of an age which is coming that will be a time of light.

We speak now of frequencies, energies and vibrational forces. Vibration, as you know, is what creates sound for you. There are frequencies that the human ear cannot hear, for they are either too high or too low. Indeed there is a limited amount that you do hear. Now, it is important that you discover the possibilities of sound, for at present you hear just the sound. The vibration - that you cannot hear. Again we repeat, science and intuition will merge.

It is important for you to have stillness. It is not good, and never has been good for you to have noise constantly inflicted upon you. You cannot realise just how much damage noise has done to you. It has acted as a block in your minds. The noise of machinery, vehicles and even your music can damage you. In some music there are frequencies which can inspire you. Each person has their own note. This cannot be heard, but a few can sense it. Some sounds harmonise with your own note, and are joyous and expansive for you. This is why some people find music discordant and others enjoy it. Be selective which music you listen to, particularly now, when all energies are being enhanced from the Source. You need stillness, peace and solitude, not twenty four hours a day, but a little every day. The fact that you cannot hear everything is a safety valve, but

11

now that some of you are experiencing heightened perception, certain sounds will annoy and irritate you. The same sounds would not have worried you before. You can deal with this by allowing yourself a few moments in silence each day. In silence you can align and balance the energy frequencies of your individual notes. The most important thing for you to do now is to love and understand yourselves.

Every little leaf, each tiny insect - even your nails and hair have energy. Think for a moment about your plants. You can see the energy in a leaf which has been picked off a tree. You can watch, as over a period of hours it shrivels and the energy leaves. Energy is never destroyed. The energy from the leaf goes back into the earth, and so it is with the physical body. You do not die; rather you transmute, physically to the earth, emotionally to the astral. The soul lives on to expand and grow. *There is no death.*

The energy of the Earth is slightly different. Over the years structures change, blend and metamorphose. Now your scientists, using intuition, will have a much clearer understanding of your planet Earth than before. And in understanding the structure and substance of your home planet, you will begin to truly understand the Cosmos and the Universe. Then, you will be able to play a greater part in it.

So many times we have said to you that you are not alone. How many of you *really* understand this? Again, we paint a picture, of electricity running from a plug to an iron or to a television. These items are separate and have different purposes, and yet the source which powers them and enables them to work is the same. Now can you see what we mean when we say that you are not alone?

12

Every individual has to expand, and does so through experience. There are very, very few individuals who have a lifetime without expansion. All, even the hard in mind and spirit, those who seem dead to the life force, to the beauties and the wonders of the world, expand in their own way.

Now, at this time, there is an electric charge running through you all. This is coming from the Source. This charge is exhilarating and expansive. It will not last forever, it will last but a few years. Take this opportunity of greater energy, dear children of light, which is here to help you break all boundaries. It is here to help mankind expand and become greater spiritual beings.

The energy you have within is a vibrant spiritual force. This energy is tapped into the Source, and you have a wonderful opportunity for the enlargement of your whole being. So we say again dear children, we *implore* you to take this opportunity.

II. ENERGIES & MAGNETISM

There is a lattice of swirling energies moving within and around your globe. Every thought process, every feeling, every action that you take has, and creates an energy. Most humans are groping in the darkness seeking futile goals, in the hope that this will lead to happiness. The only true goal is to move closer to, and eventually combine with, the fountainhead of light, the God-Source. Everything else that you do is but a reflection of this goal.

Material things might give you some limited satisfaction, a feeling of gaining something, such as position, money or power. What you are really striving for is to move up the ladder, closer to the Godhead. So, relative to this, as you seek to manifest a reaction in the material world, you might think you want to be at the top of your tree, but when you achieve this you find that after a moment of pleasure, the pleasure fades. This is because the soul light within tells you there is more. You realise that what you have striven for is not enough. Most of you then continue to push, jumping from one thing to another - and still you are not satisfied! However, in the process of pushing forward in whatever you do, a positive energy is created along with its counterforce in the Universe. Then, through the experience of pushing forward, you can notice this reflection in the Universe. And once you reach the very top or the very bottom, depending on your individual character and personality, enlightenment can come.

14

When you experience love through the emotions, much energy emanates from you. This energy is emotionally scintillating, and shoots out into the atmosphere like sharp little needles that irritate rather than stab. This irritation is felt by yourself and by those who come close to you. In desiring this love you are really desiring union with the Source, and when you find what you describe as true love, this is again but a reflection of the love and fulfilment that you will eventually find when you return to the Source. There are many forms of what you call love. The truest form, however, in human terms, is the love of friendship, the opening up to another person when there is neither demand nor control over the other. This is the truest image, a mirror of God. When you get enmeshed in emotion, the passion, desiring, wanting and the jealousy that you feel sends out black energy which is very similar to hate and fear. Think on this: negative vibrations are thrown out, all of which must go somewhere - they either stay within the aura of the individual concerned, creating problems for them, or they shoot out into the astral realms in the form of negative black cloud energies. This process is now coming to an end, for the astral has to clear. It is now clearing, and in the future it will no longer exist.

You have within your bodies different energy frequencies. The energy of the soul is a separate force within your body. It motivates you even though you are not always aware of it. It is stronger than the physical, emotional and mental energies. It motivates you, and as we explained earlier, most of those who are materially based find a reflection of it in the material world. All energies within the body originally emanated from the Source. The emotional

15

centres are there to enable you to perceive and learn compassion for your fellow man. Unfortunately, fear energy very often transmits a frequency to the emotional body that stirs and sparks it. And once the emotions are sparked in a negative way, they can perpetuate themselves, causing untold damage to yourself and others.

To quieten this emotional frequency, thought patterns must come from the mind to still it. It cannot be stilled by its own energy. Always, the higher frequencies tap on the door and say "Enough!". Then, at the point of release, the restless negative energy will dissipate. There is, however, a better way to quieten this negative force, and it is one that has hitherto rarely been used, but it can be utilised now. Instead of using a mental switch to turn it off, you can touch and expand your soul stillness. In stillness and quietness a balance can be found. We now expect more and more of you to do this. This can also be used as a way of stilling the mind. Negative mental energy must also be stilled. It cannot be stilled by its own energies, it can only be quietened by the soul - the highest force.

Emotional energy can create more astral energy, or it can stay within the individual's aura, or cling to another's aura. Some observers and healers can see auras, and can see how negative astral energy damages the aura. It is no good blaming others for your negativity. Astral energy, like any other, ebbs and flows with its magnetism. And where there is suffering, there is always some dark energy which has been drawn in; the person in question has allowed it in.

If you break this circuit using your soul stillness,

your pain will be released. If you think on this, you will see how important it is to have a clear point of resonance within yourselves, and if you do, then pain will end. It is important that you begin now to understand how energies and magnetism really work in the Universe.

The desire to reach the highest state of love is within every human soul. High perfected love, like everything else, is an energy. Love, in all its facets, is a vibrational frequency. Only through expanding the soul, by unfolding the darkness of the image, can the individual begin to hear and attune to perfected love. Perfected love is not emotional. It is the frequency of light. Eventually, even the highest love frequency will be transcended, but this need not concern you now - this will occur during further evolutions in the future.

Again we say, nothing remains stagnant and nothing ever will. This is a daunting concept for you to realise - that there is no beginning and no end. Mutation, transformation, growth and dispersals - all the time everything is moving. There was, of course, a physical beginning to your planet and there will be a physical end, but there will never be an end to the energy of your planet. This will transmute and grow. A major cosmic cycle is now coming to an end. The Cosmos is always moving, shifting and reformulating, at this time to great effect. Man has but a few years left to disconnect from what you call karmic forces. So a great deal has to be worked through, both on an individual and at a global level.

Every living thing is feeling an acceleration. It is natural that the karmic principle on your globe should come to an end. There is a movement forward at a Cosmic level, a transformation. Yours is but one mind in a Universe of minds, one cell in the whole. Cells mutate and grow and die. Your planet is not dying, it is mutating. You are mutating. You are experiencing very different energy frequencies now. Something similar happened many millions of years ago, but this was not the same - the present mutations occurring on Earth are something different and new.

The beings who first stood on your planet brought energy that accelerated growth, because the conditions at that time were right for growth. This was used to accelerate plant life, and to infuse more energy into animals, so as to enlarge them. It was not known which animals would be able to take this acceleration and complete this transmutation. Some species could not take this energy of a heightened frequency, and died out.

The most adaptable creatures were the apes. Energy of higher frequencies surged into them, accelerating their evolution. The beings who were assisting with this process were higher forces, helpers in the Universe. As always, the higher lifting the lower. As this infusion of energy occurred, apeman changed, mutated and grew, all within a very short space of time. Many scientists still believe the process of apeman becoming modern man took millions of years, but this is not so. The cranium changed, and the brain altered. The sensations, the fingers and feet; the shape of apeman changed. And now, dear children of this planet Earth, a similar mutation is taking place. You are moving on. Your bodies, feelings, thoughts and brain cells are mutating in light.

Think for a moment on the differences between cumbersome apeman, and modern man with an intelligent brain and adaptable, nimble hands and feet. Think on how much the brain has changed. And now the brain of man is changing again. Now you can begin to conceive what it is you are mutating into. Your cumbersome vehicles will become lighter. The brain will be alive with a frequency of energy that will give it its own musical harmony. The knowledge of what man is capable of, and of what he is becoming, is already beginning to permeate into the minds of some of you. Just as the change from apeman into modern man only took a short time, so it is now. This transformation has already begun, and you have only to wait a little while longer before fulfilling not just a dream, but the destiny of man.

Just as in the past there were species that could not tolerate this heightened energy, so it is now. Do not be sad for them. There are races who will disappear also, their energy will move on. Remember, there is no death. There is a form of creature not unlike your dinosaurs, which is alive and lives on a different world, many light years away.

You must now acknowledge that emotional pain is only the result of a disturbance in the emotional body. Physical pain is only to let you know when something is wrong with your physical body. But, as your brain moves and accelerates, because the body is becoming very much less important, you will eventually lose all pain on the physical level. Pain registers in the brain, and was genetically formed for a particular reason at a specific time during your evolution. But now it is of no further value to you. Emotions are also dissipating, so emotional pain will also no longer exist. You are becoming more in tune with the governing principle of compassion in the Universe. You will not need your lower emotions, they have served your growth.

Nothing we are describing here should be construed as either right or wrong, good or bad. We are simply noting that growth is taking place. You do not criticise nor destroy a bulb just because it has yet to flower. You do not state that the bulb is bad. Only by first being a bulb can a plant become a beautiful flower. You cannot have the flower without the bulb. Emotions, pain and karma are the sorrows you have experienced, and their only purpose was for your growth. Open your minds to this, open your souls and see the truth.

There is a keynote, a sound for every energy. Your physical body has a sound at a certain frequency, as do your emotions and your thoughts. We say this; your note is moving up an octave. This is not a literal statement, but a mental picture through which you can understand. Your emotions have been vibrating at a low sound frequency. And as the vibration moves higher, the coarseness of your emotions will be left behind. Those of you who understand the dynamics of sound and harmony can begin to comprehend what is happening. In one sense, as the frequency of the note is raised, the original note will no longer be heard. And, as the frequency is heightened, your awareness will rise up with it.

For some people, this transition will be disturbing. Many sounds entering your consciousness will pull at and irritate you. Go with these sounds, for they are part of the new journey. You have a saying, when your children suddenly grow faster, you say "growing pains". Mankind is having growing pains now. Is it not wonderful and a delight to see your children grow? These pains herald your emergence into adulthood. Again, we say mankind is "coming of age".

We love you because you are a part of the whole - not with emotional love. Many of you throughout the long years of your history have sensed our love. But because your love for us could only be expressed as a reflection, it was expressed through your emotions. Unfortunately these emotions created a religious fervour, and some of you became fanatical, which was destructive to many. Now, as you open up to new growth, you must not become fanatical, you must not preach.

There are many reasons why some of you will be left behind at this point of evolution. Some of these reasons are genetic. But you do have a choice. You can let go of fear and emotion if you choose.

Know that you can fly! We are not predicting you will grow feathers - you are not mutating into birds! But as your bodies become lighter, you will be able to float and glide. Also, the gravitational pull of your Earth is already weakening, so there will be less gravity, so you will be able to glide without the need of wings.

Come with us, dear children of light, and we will take you to a safe place. This is an adventure both for you and for us. And although something similar has happened to other planets, each world is unique - your planet is both beautiful and unique. We will enjoy this experience together. Put away your tears of emotion. Strive to reach up to the highest form of perfected love. Let it permeate your bodies, expanding and radiating from within you, helping all those with whom you come into contact. There is an additional frequency of energy calling you now. Begin now to see yourselves as creatures of light, because that is your destiny and what you will become.

III. JUMPING THE VORTEX

We greet you with open arms as your energy links with ours through a union of light. Take comfort in this, not the comfort of protection, but the comfort of oneness with the whole. We shall endeavour to give you more information at a level that can now be understood by more and more people. We would not have given you this information one year ago. This information is for the use of all those who can be touched by it.

We spoke of the Earth's energies, and how they mingle with every other energy. We have already stated that man is widening his sphere of understanding and is now able to lock onto higher energy frequencies. We want to make it clear that you may not hear these frequencies, but you will nevertheless have a sense of some disturbance, a kind of knowing in the brain. Because of these frequencies some of you are experiencing sharp sensations, particularly in the head. The cells within your cranium are expanding. You know already that only a minor part of your brain is used. Now the creaky doors are being opened, stimulating other cells into action. Some of these cells were genetically implanted in you aeons ago. They are like a seed which has to wait until the right time before it can germinate. The time for germination is now.

The waters that cause the seed to stir are here within your mind. Much knowledge is coming to you now, including memories of past times, prehistoric times. Some of you can see strange images which you do not understand, images of times long ago. And yet this is not entirely alien to you. You feel comfort when you see these pictures, because they are like photographs which remind you of a former home. Even now, some of this information is not so foreign to you, for we speak of a time when, in your terms, there were star beings of light upon Earth who helped to promote growth upon your planet. You have no written history or proof of this, and yet you know this to be true. Once again these beings, these energies have come close to you. And coupled with the seeds that are already germinating in your minds, there is new information, energy and power which is being made available to you.

In a very short space of time, you will have physical and tangible contact with beings from other worlds. These beings will be in your rooms, you will see them, you will touch and speak to them; they are coming to comfort you. The beings we speak of are beings of light, humanoid in feature, and yet not human. They are translucent beings. And when you meet them, you will see in them your own evolutionary destiny. Very few of you, not even those who are less evolved, will doubt the changes and the shifts that are now taking place. These light beings we speak of will give you information which you will need to protect human life energies from the storms that will occur on your planet. Did you know, dear children, that your planet is no longer revolving as it once did? Its axis is shifting, and this will create many changes.

These beings each have a sound frequency or note, which together create a harmony. In your case, your individuals notes are different from those of every other being. We speak of this note, because there is a harmonic adjustment occurring whereby higher beings, such as yourselves, are raising your notes to synchronise with those of others of your kind. When there are many of you present, and this synchronisation takes place, a harmonisation will occur that will automatically bind you together, and give you a resonance of power, similar to the resonance of the star beings we speak of. They have a unity of resonance within themselves, across a dynamic range of frequencies.

The new heightened vibrational frequencies which are growing within humans at this time are already causing disturbances inside your physical bodies. These are also creating disturbances in some of those who are close to you. These frequencies are adjusting. You will not hear them as a sound, but you will be aware of them within yourselves. You are developing a clarity, a perfect link to light. When we say perfect, we do not mean you have reached the highest possible level. You are still evolving. Your note will help you to unlock your immediate future, like the key to a door. Some of you will see and feel your bodies change, as these beings of light draw close to you. For many, many years your Earth has been free of interference. You were left alone to deal with your karmic energies in a way that was right for you.

You have had guides on the astral plane for a very long time. This particular shift is also causing changes on the astral level. This is very hard to explain in terms which are simple, and yet it is so very simple. These changes are leading to growth and to harmony with light. This change is very different to the one which happened before, because you are generating frequencies which are higher in ratio than those which were present during the shift in prehistoric times. There is nothing in your own evolutionary pattern to mirror it by.

Sound frequencies are vibrating, lifting, pulling, gently probing and pushing you upwards. There are dangers with this, for as this shift of frequencies takes place, the astral plane that was created many aeons ago is coming to an end. Within the astral, light and dark forces have constantly been at loggerheads. As individuals and humanity *en masse* make this transition to a higher frequency, disconnected from the astral planes, there is a point of departure where the negativity and dark forces close in around remaining individuals, places or groups. This is almost unavoidable. It is like jumping over a vortex, for in the process of jumping this vortex, there is a danger that some will fall. This has nothing to do with the integrity of an individual, a group, or humanity as a whole. And in the longer term, the dark forces cannot, in your terms, win - and they know it. They know that the forces which are clearing and resonating with the perfect light of attunement are far greater than their own. But despite this, they are reluctant to dissolve, and will linger where they can. This means that many individuals will have negative energies around them. These will manifest as fear, or even as entities. The period we are speaking of is now. Later, when this point of departure has occurred, there will no longer be any difficulty.

As always, the dark forces will be dissolved in light. And as many of you have trained in this work, particularly those of you who work with the astral level, you will be able to alleviate and dissolve these

26

forces of darkness. You are needed now. We emphasise this not because we are predicting blackness or evil. We have spoken much about negative forces, and we hope now that you understand what these really are. So you have much work to do. There are many groups who feel the time is now right for them to do what you define as rescue work, and indeed it is rescue work that they do. It is good that so many of you, both in this lifetime and in previous lifetimes, have trained, and now know how to work on the astral level. You may notice that at this time you are doing more of this work. Individuals must find their own perfected frequency, a new frequency that resonates with the frequency of light and sound. Although you will not resonate with the same note as the Source, you will find harmonics of this note which you can link to. Indeed, while you are in your bodies, you can never resonate at exactly the same frequency as light.

We have spoken of the difficulties that will occur during this time of transition. Unfortunately some of these will manifest in spiritual groups. Some are nothing to do with this transition, they are merely the normal irritations which occur when people work together. But some difficulties are a direct result of the shifts in frequency. Buildings have a certain note. At the point of departure, at the time when some people have jumped the vortex and others have not, there will be many difficulties. If every person in an organisation or group was prepared to work with the individual light notes of all the others, there would be no difficulties.

By sounding an audible note you can, by mirroring with sound, lift your frequencies. The sound you make is not exactly *the* note, but the idea of reaching

27

the note is the important factor here. Harmonising with the note will create a thought process, which will have a positive effect upon you.

In mass terms this will be an uncertain time for you, but in individual terms this will not be so. You will see groups of people, indeed humanity as a whole, queuing up to jump the vortex. Once over, once connected, this connection cannot be destroyed. But, whilst there are amongst you those who have yet to make this leap, the purity of your note will be brought into question by others. Because of the way the human mind works, and because of personality, some individuals amongst you may become confused, and this may cause them to doubt. But the note is so permanent once this leap has been taken, it is impossible for it to diminish. Those who believe they have lost their note will merely be having doubts. Of course, in any transition to any new level, there will always be difficulties. This transition is so great, it will cause you many difficulties. But once harmony with the dynamic frequency of the Source has been established, this cannot be diminished.

All the chakra centres are still vibrating, but energy is being pulled from the lower centres into the higher ones, with only just enough energy left in the base centre to keep you alive in physical terms - to completely deplete the lower centres would mean physical death. In the past, up until the present time, a great deal of energy from the lower centres was used for survival. These energies are moving upwards. You still have your all your chakras, but the lower ones, particularly the two base centres, are not emanating the same amount of energy they once were. When you speak of balancing the chakras, you no longer need as much physical energy in the lower

28

centres. However all of the energy of the base centres is still with you. This is rising and mingling with other frequencies to help them with their work. Even the solar plexus is gradually being shut off. In winter, when there is not enough power from the sun's rays to warm you, you turn on your boiler. But in summer, when the sun is exuding more heat, you turn it off again, as the boiler's heat is no longer needed. And so it is with the chakras. There will be a turning off, to conserve energy, and to transmute it into areas which are more vibrant. You will notice this in healing work. You will find that some people have what you consider, at present, to be normal energy. But if you touch and give healing to those who have made this leap we speak of, you will perhaps be perturbed by the lack of energy that you find in their lower centres. Do not confuse this lack of energy with a health condition. You must recognise this condition for what it is.

There is much work to be done on the chakra centres of the heart and throat, because the energy is, as it were, pumping through the heart. Some people have experienced an extra heartbeat. Indeed there is an extra heartbeat, although this does not emanate from the physical heart, but from the heart chakra centre. As you know, the positions of the chakras do not exactly correspond to the organs. At this time there is a surge of energy moving into the heart centre, transmuting its frequency. The same is also happening to the other higher centres. The rusty doors are opening.

If you examine a piece of limestone and observe the patterns in the rock, you can get a sense of the history of the stone. But because of the changes of frequency that are now occurring, rocks, trees and everything that exists on Earth are resonating with a different frequency. This will break up some existing structures, and literally turn them into lumps of stone. Perceptive people can hold a piece of rock and sense the changing frequencies. You can literally feel the shift that is occurring within the stones, and because the earth underneath your feet is also changing, this is creating some discordant notes during this period of transition. As yet, your scientists have not done enough work on sound and vibrational energies. If they had, they would know of and be able to measure these changes.

Man has taken his planet for granted. He can no longer continue to do this because Earth is crying out for a higher note. Your Earth cries out in the way that your own soul cries out, with the desire to move forward. The changes in Earth's energies, together with the changes in the frequencies from above, are creating lightning-like flashes of force which are disturbing your atmosphere. Your atmosphere is charged with energy forces and is changing. Even as we speak, changes are occurring.

There is an energy point above the heart which registers the soul light. This point is closer to the heart than to the throat. This soul essence is now being disturbed. We do not use the word disturbance negatively, but as a descriptive word. The soul light of individuals is pushing and forcing its way out. Perceptive healers and other perceivers of energy can experience this as a flame. This is because it generates much energy. When something shifts, it creates heat and generates more energy. This is like the flames of a fire which roar when it first gets going. But when the fire settles, the flames die down. This picture is inadequate, but one which you

30

may understand. Because so many of you have worked to uncloak the light force, it is in one sense leaping with vibrancy. This is exciting, a wonderful thing for you, not a negative thing. Not long ago your soul energy was located just under your heart, above the solar plexus. For some time now, it has been moving higher. It will of course move up further, but this need not concern you now.

Healers in particular will have a touch which feels like an electrical charge, and they can use this to operate on people. These forces will reach into the body like a laser beam, and dissolve tumours, cancers and similar kinds of physical disabilities. You can sense these forces, you will be able to see them.

Teachers also will use their own note, which will automatically raise the notes of others - if they are ready for this. You must trust yourselves, for it is not your words which do the teaching. You will know when the words you speak are the right ones. The less evolved ones will need words, and you will speak these words to them. Your words act as catalysts, and are all that is needed to trigger an individual to open up. It is the *energy* of the teacher, or the leader which really makes a difference. There are now more teachers and leaders than there have ever been before, and they are sorely needed. Have no doubt that those whom you lead into the "garden of paradise" will connect with you, for it is your energy and vibration that is really doing the work. Your trust in oneness makes you complete. You hear the note within your head. You feel the pull, the connection. Do the work that is your destiny. We will leave you today with that thought.

IV. INITIATIONS

We have spoken of a wind of change, which is a movement of energy. The astral body of your Earth is moving rapidly: dark forces in its astral body are holding on. There is, in your terms, a sharp piercing note entering the astral body of the Earth from above. This has begun already. This piercing note is dissolving the dark forces. It is like a laser beam of light, a high-frequency note dispelling all negative forces that it comes into contact with. This is very difficult to explain, but if you can paint a mental picture of a flash of lightning, a sharp laser beam coming into and stimulating your Earth, you will have some idea of what we are saying. At present this note is entering in at a single point, and as Earth revolves, this point moves with it. This point is located in the Northern hemisphere, somewhere between the landmass you call Greenland and the island which you call Ireland.

The astral body of the Earth has expanded over many aeons, but now it must contract. The astral body affects the physical, and this is why your scientists have not quite mastered the laws of gravity. The missing link is the astral, which affects the physical. When your scientists realise this, their calculations, which describe the solar system, will be complete. There is work now being done to stimulate the minds of scientists on your planet, those who can accommodate this information. Light, power and information is being channelled to those whose specific duties are to integrate science into the New Age. Of course some of this information crosses the boundaries of different disciplines, and that is quite as it should be. There will be a link between those who can read and understand this new material and those who need the scientific papers now being drawn up. This material speaks to those who understand on an intuitive level, and to those of you who have journeyed inwards and have taken initiations in the past.

The astral body of your Earth is diminishing, and as a result the negative forces around your globe are, as it were, fighting for their very existence. They are trying to establish a foothold in some countries, organisations and individuals. Never before have the beings of light on the astral level had so much work to do. At this time all beings of light are being called to action. In the past some of them have dedicated themselves to channelling information to particular mediums. Some of these will have to leave the individuals with whom they are in contact, because all beings of light on the astral level are needed now. Much work has already been completed to ensure that negative astral energy from below - from humans - will not seep back into the astral body of the Earth. Much work is being carried out to ensure the opposite does not occur, that dark forces are prevented from seeping back into the Earth. Similar gatherings of light beings have occurred in the past, but never has there been such a union of angel beings, with golden radiance, protecting and dissipating, transmuting the darkness, so that your planet will transform and follow its evolutionary destiny, to become a planet of light.

Nothing has gone wrong. Many people have asked

the question, "Where is God?", "Why have we been deserted?". You have never been deserted. And now, as you spiritually come of age, you realise that your pain and your experiences have made you grow strong. You are veritable rocks of light.

When we speak of influences which are coming in now, these are different from the divine sources which some of you have always had the ability to link to. Your planet is being energised. Its frequency note is rising. Would that you could hear the harmonics of the universe and see the patterns which they create. When a planet is going through intense difficulties, it becomes discordant with the Universe, and when that discordant note is heard, help is sent. Now this is not the case with your planet. The energy which is being sent to you now is not because you are sounding a discordant note. It is coming at the present time because the wheel has turned full circle, and the time is now right for the point of light to enter again, as it did many thousands of years ago when, as we said in an earlier session, mankind made the transition from animal to modern man.

Obviously it is impossible for us to describe in words the frequencies and notes which we are endeavouring to explain to you, for these are sounds, and therefore cannot be described in words or written down. But if you mentally open the cells of your body to these frequencies, some of you will be able to hear an echo, a reflection of the sound, of the harmonic structure of the Universe.

In terms of your units of years and months, it is not possible to pinpoint the exact time of entry of this point of light, but know that this light has already entered. Its presence was sensed some years back and it finally entered a few months ago. Gathered around this point are beings of energy that are comparable to what you describe on your planet as devas. These energies are like fire creatures, elated salamanders. They guide and protect the etheric essence of light, just as your devas concern themselves with the etheric essence of your plants, and some with that of yourselves. Even now you do not understand that there are many facets, beings and energies, which are not human, which serve their purpose in the evolutionary process of your world. Some of you sense them, and a very few of you perceive some of them, but none of you perceive all of the energies that make up the whole. Every being, every frequency, every energy has its work to do.

Because of disturbances in energies, you will notice that machinery, particularly machinery that is connected with or powered by fire or electricity, will tend to go wrong. There will be more than just the usual occasional breakdowns. Even your motorised vehicles will be affected through their electric systems, and it would be as well for you not to possess vehicles that rely upon electrical controls. You may also notice that more than the usual amount of fires will start. These will have many different causes, or so it will be assumed. In fact these will be caused by the vibrational frequencies which are now coming in. You will note these over the next few months, as once again humanity as a whole dismisses these coincidences as chance occurrences.

We must emphasise that it is not our intention to instil fear into you, nor that you should anticipate a fearful time to come. We are endeavouring to do the opposite. We are trying to throw light onto matters which will assist with the expansion of your minds. We only make reference to these matters because they are of interest to you, we do not intend that you should find them fearful. If the more sensitive of your animals could speak, they would tell you that something is stirring. In particular dogs, elephants and dolphins are amongst the most sensitive of creatures. They have always been attuned to humanity and to the frequencies of Earth as a whole.

We speak now to your hearts. Be firm, dear children of light, be as rocks, be solid in your strength. Those of you who have yet to "jump the vortex", continue, continue, continue to work on erasing your inner darkness, knowing that you have the strength of diamonds. And for those of you who have jumped the vortex, keep that rocklike strength within. Even though this cannot be diminished, you can become irritated, if you allow it. What wondrous, vibrant sounds are emanating from you as more and more of you take this step, this jump. We speak to you of angel beings of light, but the angels alone cannot force you to make this jump. But every time a soul makes this jump, they can automatically link to the angels both above and below, so that you correspond to the unity of all, and to the note that furthers and pushes forward the evolution of mankind: joyous times are coming.

As you know, initiations have occurred before, and sometimes they occur within in a group. But it is not always possible, nor relevant, for a whole group of people to be brought over the vortex during an initiation. However, there will be a few occasions when this kind of initiation will happen en masse, but this will only happen to specific people in specific places. Most initiations are carried out on an individual basis at this time, perhaps through being awakened by another radiant soul. When you use the word initiation, this is not an accurate description, for it is not the same as the initiations of the past. In bygone times, initiations were rigidly structured. This was because of the limitations of the methods available to individuals at the time, and because of the way the initiates responded. The current initiation processes are unstructured: what occurs is the same, but without the ritual.

Rituals are not relevant at this time. Symbols that permeate the mind can be useful both to leaders and to pupils, but not rituals or structured formats. In one sense, these initiations will happen automatically, for you will remember that we spoke of how initiates are attracted to light beings who can help. Never doubt that those who need a particular impetus or climactic occurrence in order to trigger their initiations will, at the appropriate time, be drawn to light individuals, and their initiations will occur. You are aware no doubt, that there are many high priests and priestesses around today. Not all of them will have sufficient strength, and unfortunately not all of them, who have reincarnated at this time, will be able to further their work, but many of them will.

We give you the name Siaphas, which is not to be confused with Sirius. Siaphas was an extraordinarily powerful being, a master of masters, dominating the energy at one time in your planet's history. Now Siaphas' energy is with you again, not in one person, but in many.

Unfortunately, some reincarnated priests and priestesses have gone beyond themselves and have become consumed with pride, thereby rendering their work useless. It is the quality of humility within powerful beings which gives them solid strength and makes them great. Many powerful beings are overly concerned with what they have to do. They believe they should be standing up on podiums, shouting their message: they should not. Trust, you beings of light, that the light itself is your teacher, your magnetism and your strength.

Everything is happening in the present, and you must work with the present, with what is around you. You are where you are meant to be, and you are doing what you are supposed to do. Memories of past times are with you only because you have opened up to them. They are helpful to some extent, but they are not necessary for your work. Concentrate on today. All is one. All is one time. All is one breath. One day you will experience the loss of your body and total immersion within the Oneness.

Have you ever lain on the ground and looked through the leaves of a tree at the sun? Have you ever looked at the crystal reflection of the sunlight shimmering on water? The sunlight breaks up into separate points of light, and yet you know it comes from a single source. Think on that. Picture this image, and you will understand, allow it to touch your hearts.

All things are important, and when we speak of "the little ones", this is not a derogatory statement, no more than if we were to refer to your children as little beings. There is always the potential for endless growth, of which both you and we are aware.

You are already working with dolphins and other animal friends. They have their own sources of protection, their own beings, and their own connections with the Source. You, as human beings, must not interfere with this, although you can communicate with them by thought and by touch. They have their own point of reference to the Source, which is not the same as yours. Within their group soul they are singing their note loudly, the note of freedom. Some creatures are also taking a leap of consciousness in order to expand and grow. This is a wondrous thing. All beings of energy and living matter are part of the whole, different notes from a single instrument.

We are bringing this session to a close with one more thought. The spectrum of the universe is huge. You have your colours of the rainbow, which are connected to the light spectrum of your world. But the spectrum across all light frequencies is far beyond your imagining. It is wonderful and enormous, and yet this spectrum is still one. It is still linked to all the universe, and to each and every tiny cell in even the tiniest creature. Now, because this laser beam of light is entering your globe, cells and all living forces are being stimulated. Now, dear children of light, your rainbow will have many more colours, and these will enhance the opportunity you have for leaping the vortex into light.

V. GATEWAYS

Leave all your difficulties and confusions behind you now, dear children of light, and concentrate on your inner core of perfected light, your inner core of energy that is beyond any worldly influences, beyond emotions, beyond rancour - just pure Source energy within. This is where you must register your energies.

It is becoming more difficult to help the little ones, for their minds are blocked and some of them are closing even tighter. It is perhaps best not to try. Give them words of encouragement, and ask them to look at themselves. They have the answers if they choose to look within. We say with gentleness, that it is a waste of your time trying to get through when you find yourself constantly coming up against a brick wall.

There are many souls enlightening now, many sudden awakenings and revelations. Many more than at any other time. This is joyous. But, again we say to you, there is a marked difference between the little ones who remain and those who have begun their grand awakening.

Those of you who are sensitive have noticed the energy fluctuations which have occurred this year. This will continue. Energy will continue to come in, not constantly, but in influxes of light. This is affecting the molecules of your bodies. The molecular structure of the physical body is beginning to change.

A metamorphosis is taking place, and the sensitive ones among you will feel this. Of course everyone will feel it differently, but most of you will feel it in the head, the throat and in the glands: in the lymph and the pineal glands in particular. This should not create illness, but it will create some disturbance. We are having some difficulty, in that there are those of you who need and want more information about these changes. But some of this information is hard for you to comprehend, and to some it seems negative. We say to you clearly that change is constant, and the changes which are now taking place are positive, for mankind is lifting its consciousness beyond the state of karma, awakening into true spirituality.

Your planet has but a few years left of karma. This is a reality. Humans will no longer have to experience the kind of difficulties which you have encountered. And so a clearing is taking place, which is physical as well as spiritual. There is a cosmic change of *physical* energies taking place. This is a reality, no matter what interpretation you try to give it. A physical cosmic change is taking place which no one can alter. This change does not depend upon karma, or on being good or bad. This change is occurring, and it cannot be stopped. It is real.

The spiritual hierarchy of guides is very active at this time. They do not often interfere, as they are, for the most part, watchers and guardians of the Earth. Rarely in the past have they intervened, and then, only in times of necessity. At this time they are sending master knowledge down to Earth, because Earth is now in need of this. Master knowledge is entering the consciousness of many people who live upon your globe. It is entering the consciousness of many who do not even realise it. The book of

41

knowledge has been opened in a way that has never happened before, and many among the mass of humanity are now picking up this information. Some are misinterpreting it. Most, however, are disregarding it. But those of you who have risen in consciousness know of the reality of the changes, and know that you must keep a stillness within. Your planet is undergoing a change of mammoth proportions, such has never before been encountered in the whole of human history. You know of nothing with which you can compare it. This knowledge of your soul is very new to you. Lift your minds for a moment out of your planet, out of your solar system, into the Cosmos. Worlds are being created every day, new suns are being born, old suns are dying. There is constant change throughout the universe, and in cosmic terms, the changes which Earth is experiencing are really not that great. Your planet is metamorphosing. You can easily see how some who have encountered this knowledge could misinterpret it, and believe that the planet is dying. Your planet is not dying, it is changing. The human race is not dying, it is metamorphosing. And at any time of change that means physical deaths will occur. This is nothing new. You speak of Armageddon. This is *not* Armageddon. It is as if a caterpillar were changing into a butterfly.

You speak of negative and positive, you speak of male and female. Positive qualities, negative qualities, male and female qualities; neither of them is right or wrong, good or bad. These qualities are simply different.

Your planet is moving into a different sphere of consciousness. You are moving away from the material to the spiritual. That which is not needed

42

for the new growth will disappear. You can see this happening, for on your planet upheavals are taking place even as we speak. These are movements and shifts of energy. Soon, there will be another huge intake of energy. You will see this for yourself. Listen to the consciousness of the world. Listen, and you will hear the heartbeat of the world. And through the heartbeat of the world you will be in contact with the hierarchy of planets. Through the sound, you will hear the heartbeat of the world.

There are beings who are still watching and guiding you. They are still teaching, giving you a crammer course of knowledge. Some of this knowledge you have known before, some of it is very new. These beings are the guardians of the planet, giving initiations to those who have truly uncloaked the soul. This use of their energy will be over in but a few short years, and they will move on to another time and space. Many of you have been aware of their teaching. They are the last links on the higher astral planes.

Many of you are aware that the cells in your brain are opening up to this new knowledge. Your mind has not yet assimilated all this knowledge, but it is there for you when you need it. In your brain new doorways are opening, the new door of consciousness for the new energy that is coming. You have need of these gateways to consciousness, otherwise you would not survive. They are a bridge for the human body. Indeed, these new gateways will allow the divine Source to come through into a space that is clearer than ever it was in the past. It is complicated, and yet so very simple. We have tried to put this across to you very simply. We use simplistic terms, but they are nonetheless true.

These are cosmic changes which we speak of, so please do not waste time on petty matters, on the remnants of personality difficulties. Do not waste time on trying to accumulate worldly things. There is no point in this now. Just find a way to support yourselves as best as you can, and attune yourselves to the new energies. Everything else is unimportant. There is a germination of information taking place, a nucleus of light. You are about to encounter a new genesis, a new beginning, a new reality, even new truths. The father, the Source is always with you, and always will be. You can be at one now. In your meditations, sing out your note. This note is a reflection of the cosmic note of change, and it will help you to lift into the new dimension. Be at peace with yourself, for that is all the human soul has ever wanted, a peace that is beyond all understanding, a peace that reaches to its core.

As the wheel turns, the core stays the same. We speak now of the gentle peace which you have so long desired. There could be no peace before, for your planet is one which has evolved as a karmic planet. To learn the laws of cause and effect you needed the interaction of positive and negative, which meant disturbance. How else could you have learnt to see the light, other than through its shadow? Peace was never meant to be on your planet, but now there will be peace. These physical changes would have happened whatever you had done. But blissfully some of you have grown. Not many, in proportion to the number of souls which have come onto your planet, but some of you have grown. So now some of you can take this leap of consciousness, and in making this leap you will find your peace. You have your stillness. And from this point of stillness, nothing else matters. It is circular, it is

44

nothing and it is everything.

You are free. You are no longer trapped in the bonds of karma. Light forces, gentle rains of light are pouring down upon you. You are free, and in that freedom you will automatically help others by using your energies. You will help without thought of yourselves. There is work to be done, which you will do, and you can help others in other times and in other spaces.

Hold tight, dear children of light, because your planet is also taking this leap. There are more changes to come in the material world. More changes of leaders. People in power will be replaced, and these again by others. There will be changes of regimes, changes in the atmosphere, changes of temperature, changes everywhere. The structure of the Earth is moving, and you are moving too.

Look ahead of you, and you will see a gateway, an unfamiliar doorway. This doorway is filled with a strange bright light. You are entering now. Physically, mentally, spiritually. For some, the change is just too much, a shock to the body, mind and soul, so you may see sudden unexplained deaths. You will be charged with new frequencies. You will have your own eternal source of light, self perpetuating. Your bodies will be lighter, and will eventually become translucent; you will need less food, and you will gain your energy directly from the sun and from the light rays. You will need some food and water, but most of your energy will come from a kind of photosynthesis, a constant source of nourishment. Your bones will change. A reaction has already started which will make your bones strong and hard as rock. You will notice this first in and around the jaw bone. You will not be able to break your bones, for they will become like granite. You wanted this information and so we are giving it to you now. You have asked in truth and it has been given in truth. You can deny it, for that is your right, but you will see it for yourselves, and know it to be true. You are one with the Universe, and when you take this leap, you transcend the need for a home, for a globe, for an Earth. Transcend that, and you will no longer have any desire for security. You will want to be in other places in order to be of service, not just for the service of humanity, but for service for the Cosmos. Think on that, and do not fear.

All is happening as it should.

VI. THE MIND OF GOD

You are still sons and daughters of the Universe. You each have your own particular rhythm, your note, and you can attune yourself to the universal song. The ebb and flow, the breathing in and the breathing out, are a total reality. You are all part of this. This is not something that the intellect can absorb, it is a reality much truer than the illusions you create in your own world of personality. We do not come to you to preach. We speak only to those who will listen. Whether you listen or you turn your back, the reality, the universal force, will still be there. For some of you now, an awareness of the hugeness of the changes is entering your consciousness. But most of you still cast a veil across your minds. It is not easy, but not impossible for you to understand, or to want to understand. We do not make predictions. We simply comment on what is occurring. So please lose your fear, and find your stillness within.

The energies of your planet are gradually moving and shifting. Remember your planet is a living, breathing planet. You could say poetically that it is giving birth. It is in the throes of birth pains, and is moving and thrashing about. You can see signs of this in disturbances such as earthquakes, in winds and in storms. Earth is giving birth to a new force. There is a season and a time for everything, and your time of pain is nearly over. Very few of you have realised the wonderful potential of your green planet.

Yours has been a planet of opportunity and growth, but so few of you have realised its potentials. Most of you have only ever homed in on the pain and the suffering. We have spoken much of the negative energy these thoughts have created, which have, in consequence, perpetuated the pain and the suffering.

As the Earth shifts, its energy also shifts, and that in itself creates change. Your energies are changing and so are your bodies. The electrical flow of your nervous system is changing, and in a sense it is becoming less active now. As new nerve fibres are created, the old are closing off. A huge amount of activity is taking place in the brain, which is serving new frequencies that are creating new forces, new flows and new nerves in your body. This is why some of you have felt tingling sensations in your extremities. This is caused by new and unused nerve fibres in your body which are coming to life. This effect will only be felt by those of a sensitive nature, and then not all of the time, only in bursts. Others, who are less sensitive, will continue to function normally, but their energy is depleting. They will not be aware of this, and they will continue to go about their day to day business. Their energy will diminish until the time of their natural physical death, when the remnants of their soul light will move on.

Electrical charges are entering the skull and brain, creating new nerve fibres. Your eyes, the senses, your touch, your sense of balance - in all these things you will find some disturbance. For example; your sense of balance may occasionally become disturbed; at times your eyesight may become blurred; and your sense of smell may come and go. These senses are being re-adjusted, and all of them will develop new sensations: a new sight; new smell; new taste and a new touch.

Man's spirit is now moving up to greater heights. And those of you with insight, those who know there is a different and better way, will go with that surge, and will fly higher and higher. Evolution does not stop, dear children, it moves on, and every now and again, for one reason or another, there is a new surge forward. Look upon this time as a huge surge of evolutionary forces, pushing you on, enabling you to fly.

Your organs need to be strong now, your heart and lungs in particular, for your heart has to pick up the new vibrating rhythms, and your lungs have to breathe in the impulses which permeate the air which you breathe. The atmosphere is becoming charged and stimulated with particles of light. As you breathe in, these particles physically expand your lungs. Your feet must also become stronger, and they will begin to broaden, for the root chakra will be relocated into your feet. This is the root connection to the new energies of your planet Earth. Another major centre will be located at the back of your skull. This is not for second sight, but for heightened sight and perception, and will be used for seeing new colours as the spectrum of your rainbow expands.

There will be two other energy points within the skull which will be important for the flow of energy. These will be located on either side of the base of the skull, forming a triangle of force. Impulses will move around these energy points very rapidly. There will be two further points on the skull, which together with the others will create the shape of an

"H". Because of the way they interact, these points will create a current which will flow between them. They will touch and harmonise with the new forces of light, like an aerial, an enhancer of the impulses.

You will still have an aura, but you will no longer have an astral body. This means that eventually you will need no sleep, because the purpose of sleep is primarily to rejuvenate the astral body. Not having an astral body will also make your perception clearer. You will have a clearer sense of reality. Your auric emanations will hum, sounding a note that interacts with others, and it is this sound vibration that will create the unison of love. There will be a type of love between two people which you have never encountered before. The feeling between two people with harmonious frequency rates is something far beyond anything you could imagine.

This love is not in any way emotional. It is a vibration at a frequency which creates pure harmonics as you interact with others. This is love. It may sound strange to you. At present what you experience as love is mainly emotions; needs, desires and wants. And in the past even the best of love has required its own gratification. But this new love is pure, and it sounds the song of the Universe. After the transition you can expect to notice great changes, as great as the metamorphosis which occurs when clumsy earthbound caterpillars become butterflies. Your changes will be every bit as dramatic as these. The way you relate to others, the way you eat, the way you perceive and the way that you reason will be very different. And because of your enhanced ability to adjust your frequency to that of others, you will have access to all the combined knowledge of the world. All knowledge, both terrestrial and higher, will be at your command.

The astral plane has served its purpose, in the same way that clouds in the sky serve a purpose. Is it not better to have clearer perception, without the clouds of the astral above and below? Imagine a crystal-clear day when the light is sharp, and the colours are vibrant in the sun - this is how your perception will be. Such will be your clarity, for this is your truth.

The hierarchy energies who are here with you, are watching closely. They will remain close to the Earth until after the transition is completed.

Breathe rhythmic breaths. Fill your soul with light for a few minutes at least once a day to still the clear lake of the soul. The mountains of Tibet have long served their purpose, for within those mountains a song is being sung, the note of the world. The guardians are moving, they sense there will be a change. There is a landshift coming. New continents will be formed. New lands will rise up from beneath the water, and others will sink below. The world will find its heart again. The Earth will have a new Tibet, and a new song to join to the universal.

Some of you still see these changes as a negative occurrence. Still others believe this to be a prelude to Judgement Day. It is not, dear children of this green planet Earth, it is not. It is a new birth. Do you not rejoice and congratulate each other when there is a new birth in the family? Birth can be painful, but a new child is a joy. The universal song is getting ready to congratulate the Earth on its birth; a new baby, a new soul, and a new heart in your world.

Even some masters are giving up their energy,

giving up their connection with the consciousness, walking away, or transferring their energy to others. This is their choice, their conscious choice. Be aware, dear children, be selective. If you listen to your soul, you will know. A huge amount of work is now being done to finally release the personality, the ego. This will ensure that there will be no remnant of ego to obstruct the link with the universal consciousness, which is the mind of the Source. This is the nucleus, the core of the Source. We paint you a mental picture of the Source as a huge eye. The consciousness is the seeing part of the eye, the nucleus. And around that is the protection, the energy, the force. The nerves and the cells are allowing the consciousness to do its work. It is the consciousness you must look to now. Most of you have been charged with the source of light. Now you must experience your revelation from the consciousness of the Source. From the pupil of the eye. From the core of the energy. From the mind of God.

The mind of God thanks you, dear children, because you have played your full part in experiencing the knowledge and the truth of your planet Earth. There has never been a planet like yours, and there never will be another. Each soul that incarnated on the Earth had a choice. You chose to come into the karmic realm, with all the difficulties this presented. Willingly you came, knowing that the knowledge and the experience which you gave back to the Godhead was beyond price and worth all the pain. You think of God as a benevolent God. Indeed, God is benevolent.

Earth has been the planet of adventure, a place where the soul could experience new and marvellous adventures, for the enhancement of the spirit, and for the experience of the mind of men. It has been a nucleus, and that nucleus is the consciousness of God. And in the heart and soul of man, there has been a knowing, a link to the Source of pure light energy. Pure spirit beyond matter. In the adventure book of life, Earth is nearing the last pages. The book is coming to an end, but there will be a sequel, where your Earth will be even greener. The players in the chapters of the book will survive to live another day. Some in another place. It has been a good book, a revelation. You have shown the consciousness a heart, and for this, yours will be the kingdom, the power and the glory.

VII. THE LAWS OF THE UNIVERSE

We speak of your Earth as a green planet, one which radiates the vibrational power of green with great intensity. The profusion of energies and all the living beings on your planet are radiating this skywards, out beyond your globe. As man has evolved he has developed rockets and satellites which can penetrate right through the Earth's atmosphere. But where you have travelled beyond your atmosphere, you have also taken with you some of your negative astral energy. You are not permitted to extend the reach of your negative thoughts beyond the confines of your Earth, for this is against the laws of the Cosmos. Your domain is your planet, and to a great extent you can do what you will with it. All living beings on Earth are free to do as they wish, even to destroy themselves if they so choose. But when you reach out beyond your atmosphere, taking your negative astral energy with you, outside the confines of the gravitational pull of your planet, then alarm bells sound in the Universe. This is because you bring with you some negative thoughts and desires.

And so, because of your activities, the Universe took notice of the activities of its brothers on Earth. It noted that energy was piercing through the outer atmosphere of your globe. Provided your negativity is confined to your own planet, the integrity of Universal law is unaffected, but if this extends beyond the boundaries of your globe, this is a different matter. At a result, it became necessary to send in forces to investigate. We have already stated that intervention with planetary affairs is very rare, but now this has become necessary, and light forces have been sent in. This action is unconnected with and separate from the processes of change which are automatically taking place throughout the whole of the Cosmos, which we spoke of in "The Wind of Change".

Your negative thought processes are largely contained within the astral, and are desire based thought patterns. These would eventually have been cleared anyway, as this is necessary in order to dissipate the negative energies of you humans, for in order for your planet to take its leap into new vibrations and consciousness, it must be free of negative thought patterns.

This is something which we have spoken of many times before. Indeed, we must speak of it again. Some of you who have read and understood these words are still living lives permeated with negative thoughts. You are still involved in petty quarrels and are ruled by ego based desires. The vast majority of the human population can neither see nor understand our words, but those of you who do understand, yet carry on regardless are, through your denial, doubly responsible for your bad thoughts. This is because your acknowledgement of the truth gives you more power, so your thoughts are pushed out with greater intensity. As a consequence they will rebound on you with redoubled energy.

Some of you are denying that God is within. Some

deny this out of false humility, which is really only an excuse for not taking responsibility for this knowledge. We urge you now, more than ever before, to accept this responsibility, to be clear of the debris and the dark clouds, so that you can see the light. Is this not preferable to that which you have now? Consider an analogy with the clouds. Dark clouds create rain. Rain is necessary for flowers to grow, and every drop of rain is an opportunity for a flower to blossom. But once a flower has blossomed it needs only to be illuminated by the rays of the sun for you to see its beauty. If you are connected to pure light, you will no longer need the rain or the shadow. You will only have need of the light. We say, dear children, if you want to make this leap, you should be aware that time is running out. You must work on yourselves, and finally uncloak your soul, which is your connection to God.

As light energy enters your globe it cuts through the astral clouds. A clearing process is taking place. We have already described how energies are created out of black astral energy. Most entities now fear for their existence, and are consequently latching on to people who put out negative thoughts, and therefore act like magnets. These entities must also be cleared. If you as individuals increase the frequency and power of your vibratory note, creating a new sound, which for the purpose of illustration we shall give the name "sonic sound", then this sonic sound will be emitted wherever you travel, with a resonance which dissipates darkness and negativity.

As you remove the cloak around your soul you heighten your vibrations, which gives you a clearer connection to the Source. You can expand by means of thought processes, and through being aware of the frequency of your energy. For some, the hierarchy guides can be helpful in achieving this. This heightening cannot be achieved by those who have not first dispensed with their negativities, so there is no point in their attempting this heightening first. But if you have listened, and have heard the note - the sound within your soul, and emitted it out of your being, so that you are constantly vibrating that note, then no negative forces, or darkness of any description can enter your body or aura. You are indeed protected. You are also an instrument for clearing. We ask you to be this instrument. Do not waste your time indulging in idleness, it is important that you help those who can hear, to listen to the universal rhythms. By doing so you do more for your planet than can be achieved through any political movement. By developing and expanding your personal frequency note, you bring to your planet more living consciousness, and you add to the force behind the clearing of all negative thoughts. This will make it easier for your Earth to pass through its transition.

To put it in terms which you can understand: at present your Earth has indigestion, and a stomach ache! Unfamiliar energy has entered in, and it is churning about inside whilst Earth adjusts to its presence. You know that your human bodies are extremely adaptable; Earth is adaptable also. Earth is adapting itself to the new frequencies. This is why you are experiencing disturbances of a physical nature. Gigantic winds, rains, earthquakes and so forth will continue to occur for another year or two whilst your planet adjusts. After this, it will quieten down. When it does, the process will not be over, indeed in one sense, it will have only just begun. Having worked through this indigestion in the form of volcanoes, earthquakes and the like, Earth will start to vibrate at the new frequencies with greater clarity. Then you will see new species of plant life emerging, and after a while new creatures also.

For when the Earth is resonating at a different note, all who live on it will attune to that note. A few of you have changed your frequency already. There will be no choice in this, for all must adjust or cease to exist. The first step in the process of attunement is letting go of fear and negativity, because if these remain with you, you cannot change, you cannot move on, you cannot see. The new frequency is so different, it will be like comparing pure raindrops to acid rain.

This is a difficult time for all of you, even for those who have already made the leap. Hold steady, do not allow other people to distort what you know to be true. This is not easy, however more healers are being made available, healers who do understand the new frequencies. The base centres have little power now, and in a matter of a year or two, these will have no power whatsoever. So healers, your time is now. If you raise your energies, you can help. If you do not, you will simply remain tuned to an obsolete channel! The responsibility is yours and yet it is all one. If you do not make the leap, your energy will move on, although it will be some considerable time before it comes back in a form equivalent to a human body. For the soul, time is eternal. There is no time.

Those who do not make the transition will have their energy drawn into a unified force. Individuality will be lost, for your energy will mingle with the universal Source, to be born again. The laws of the

Universe are exact, they have no sense of good or bad, they are absolute. If you do not make this transition, the seed of your energy will again be planted in the soil, waiting to be reborn, waiting for new rains.

There is a sea of arms reaching out through the astral. Have the courage to think of the light, of truth, of golden bells, and of the hierarchy. You can pull yourselves away from the abyss even now, but you do not have long. This is not victimisation, not punishment, not moralistic judgement, neither good nor bad - this is absolute. Only when the magnet is charged can you be lifted up. These are the laws of the Universe, and no-one and nothing can change them.

Remember, within you is the power of absolute beingness, the power of pure love. Go into the power of absolute being, of the love beyond emotion. Go into light.

VIII. SILENT CO-OPERATION

We come to you in light and power, and you have felt our power to the greatest extent that you can manage. We are nudging you all forward, and pushing harder on those who have the willingness to grow in energy. When we speak of giving you power, this does not require a conscious choice on your part, for you will automatically fill yourselves with power to a level at which you can accept it. A silent co-operation of energies is constantly taking place, both on your globe and on others, on all levels with all peoples, and with all living beings.

You often speak of balance, but this is not quite accurate. You speak of the balance of good and evil. Your idea of evil as we as we have often explained, is largely associated with the astral plane around your globe, and therefore in the future there will not be an equal balance of good and evil. Indeed, you must work to dissipate evil and negativity now. We have spoken much of the deterioration and dissipation of astral negativity. The astral body will have to dissolve, but this does not mean you will lose a spiritual counterpart; that is something quite different. The astral body is created by the emotions and thought processes, and is influenced by the state of development, position and level of the soul energy. Together with the outer casing of energies, this makes up the whole of the living being. The astral body is the shadow. When you stand directly in the light, there is no shadow.

The energies are largely unseen, but they are moving all the time, whether you are aware of them or not. This process is ever-increasing. We described before an image of oil in water, watching it continuously changing shape, changing but not decreasing. Again we present this picture, for you are further along the road of understanding, and this image will have greater meaning for you, now that you have a better understanding of these energies.

The soul is always triumphant, nothing can destroy it. The heavens are open to you now, you can glide into the light force whilst you are still in your body. You have no conception of the enormity of where you can go from here. The evolutionary pattern of your being is nowhere near its fruition. There are many more experiences and mutations ahead of you. There is a constant flow of light forces - but this is too nebulous for you at this point, so we will continue to explain what is happening on your Earth.

As the astral clears, more and more light force energies can penetrate the dense atmosphere above your globe. Consequently, you are having more communications with outer energies. We spoke last time of the dangers of negative astral thoughts travelling outside your atmosphere. There cannot be communication with beings outside your planet without a clearing of the astral, for these connections can only be made between forces of light. This does not mean that every person who has received a communication from beings beyond your world is a perfect being. These connections are made between the light within that individual and the light forces outside. There will be more of these communications from now on, and your media will be full of them.

Communications are being made not just with one star or one planet, but with many. These are coming through into the consciousness of your planet, and this is made possible because of the dissipation of the dark clouds which surround your globe. If you could have seen the astral body of your planet some fifty to one hundred years ago, it would have looked like a dense, impenetrable fog. Now, at last this is being cleared by the consciousness, by the positivity and by the evolutionary light forces of individuals on your planet. How much better it is to see the sun without the clouds.

Some of you speak of dark forces in the Cosmos and Universe. Yes, there are dark forces elsewhere, but there is nothing to compare with the kind of darkness that has been surrounding your planet. We are not stating here that there is nothing so dense, or more negative, just that there is nothing which is the same. So the antennae are listening out on your globe, and the transmissions are becoming clearer. Oh the thrill of being able to hear the transmissions of light beings! The thrill, the surprise and, to some extent, the perplexity of individuals who receive these flashes of communication!

For the most part they do not speak to you in words. What transpires is that the transmissions are picked up by your minds, and are then translated into words. Sometimes people hear words, and think the beings they are communicating with are speaking their own language. This is not so. When a communication is made, this is translated into the language of the receiver by the mind of the receiver. We speak gently but firmly to you now. Be strong. Much is happening around you. Although the group connection is one of joy, you as individuals need that inner rock-like strength. You will have your doubts, but listen to your soul, listen to your own light transmitting within yourselves. You know the truth; hold fast to it, keeping silent co-operation with the God-force, with the Cosmos and with all.

Because of the energy forces of the soul and the soul's ability to connect, some human beings have made contact with other star systems, with energies other than those of your own planet. This is part of the evolutionary pattern of some individual souls. At this time you have on your planet many souls who have had a myriad of energy experiences. Some of these were in places other than on your planet. Memories of these experiences are awakening in some souls at this time. Some have energies from other places; indeed, more than there ever have been before. Again we speak of beings as part of the whole, part of the very beginning of light forces, as it was when the physical structures of the stars, planets, and all parts of the Great Consciousness came into existence. These memories are being awakened within you now. This connection is one that is meant to be, one which will enable those who make this connection to see, to communicate, to remember the wisdom, the energy and the power that they have always had hidden within them.

The changes now occurring on Earth are affecting every living being. But as all people are different, individuals are reacting to and experiencing these bodily changes in different ways. For many, what they experience is the depletion of their life force energy. Others experience their life force being stimulated, and enhanced. They have greater centres of light within. Some deaths which are attributed to natural causes, tragedies and such like, happen because on a physical level the existing life force of an individual cannot withstand the new influx of energy. It is not that the new energy is draining them dry. What happens is they cannot reach up to it, so their own life forces retreat back into the Earth.

This is not easy for you to understand, for we are explaining this rather sketchily. What we are saying is that the experience is different for each individual. Death is just a process, it is not evil; it is not bad, nor is it a judgement. It is a process of law, and the laws are absolute. Some individuals cannot take this energy, so their own energy fails, and they die. This may seem harsh and insensitive, but this is reality. There has always been physical dissolution. A person dies when their soul elects to go, not before. If the soul knows there is nothing more it can experience in that lifetime, a physical cause is manifested to end the life of that individual. The soul cannot die.

There are those who have, throughout the aeons of time, experienced, grown, and transcended the genetic flaws of astral negativity. These are now being stimulated. At the present time one part of their bodies is being stimulated most. This part is around the glands in the neck. You will feel this growth. This may cause some discomfort, but it will only last a few weeks. The lungs must also expand and grow. There must be new breath to take in new air - the new energy. The lungs are growing, and it is very important that the lungs are kept active and refreshed with air. Some of you will find certain smells and atmospheres unpleasant, but as your lungs grow and expand, you will become better able to deal with these unpleasant odours, far better in the future than at this time. The process of transition is the most difficult. You will find carbon monoxide and smoke very unpleasant at present.

You also have a capacity for the heightening of sound, something which we have spoken about before. Indeed, we have described this as sonic sound: the connection of notes in the universal harmonisation of frequencies. We say to you now that henceforward you will hear with joy.

Healers, use your fine intuition when deciding how best to heal and balance those who come to you. Trust your intuition. There will be some who come to you who are like little children, who just need comfort and calm. You cannot use the high frequencies for everyone. To do so would cause a reaction in some like blowing a fuse. We say again, the decision whether or not to make the transition is a matter for the individual's choice. It is unlikely that those who are about to make the leap will be physically ill. This is because the physical body must be strong. Those who are physically very ill are not going to make this jump over the vortex. So, where there is great physical illness, just calm your patients. Give your beauty and your love, and this will help the individual with their *own* transition.

Every living being, every soul that is incarnate at this time, has had an opportunity for growth. The hardest thing for you to move beyond or rise above is the coding that you carry in your body. To rise above this is, in a sense, going against what is natural for the body. Think on this and you will understand. Destruction was implanted within the basic structure of man in the form of the instinct for survival. As man progressed, that instinct for survival, with its once necessary destructive element, needed to mutate. There was truly a fight between good and evil. There was a tug of war, and the course of least harm was to allow this negativity into the astral body, where the astral could join up with the forces of genetic destruction. Had this not transpired, humanity would have been totally destroyed. It was known when this happened that it would take thousands of years of experience for this to finally work itself through, and so most of you reincarnated into many difficult lifetimes. The reason for this is not because you had done something wrong, but because you were allowing the opportunity for this transmutation to work through gradually, like a thorn in flesh, working its way out to the surface throughout the aeons of time.

This was not against cosmic law. It was a choice made by your planet, not a choice directed by any outside factor. The Cosmos has, in a sense, allowed this vast evolutionary process to run its course knowing that all would work out in the end, although the Source did not know what would become of Earth, or indeed, of any other planet. Dear children, you have exceeded our expectations in your experience, your knowledge and your growth. Again we speak of the joy you have given us! The joy of human, physical experience is unequalled and incomparable to that of any other planet!

But, of course, there never were any expectations demanded of you. There was a natural flow. When the flow is outwards, no consciousness can know exactly what may occur. Now, as the wheel comes full circle, the spiral has turned to the point where you are moving into light. There will, undoubtedly, be other worlds that will have similar opportunities. Indeed, there is one other planet that has karmic laws, but we do not know where this will lead, what choices they will make within the sphere of their experience.

There is a breathing out and a breathing in. And just as you breathe in the scent of flowers, you can also breathe in noxious fumes. These are all experiences, all choices in the unlimited time of the great breath. This great breath is, in your terms, vast. You cannot even conceive of it - even in your most expanded state. It encompasses the whole Universe and Cosmos, including all the galaxies and the energies within. Picture a dragon's breath, fierce and powerful, but also cleansing, clear and beautiful.

We spoke before of not allowing yourselves to become dependent upon a crutch, and this applies also to your astral guides. There is, as we have said, a group of ascended souls, master energies, at your disposal for teaching and for your growth. There is no capacity within these energies for making excuses. They speak frankly, even bluntly, but always wisely, always with love. You must now get in touch with the consciousness within your body, for this consciousness is linked to the greater heart of the Great Consciousness. We spoke earlier of the eye, the pupil of the Source. It is not easy for your minds to understand this. Just know in your soul that it is part of the Great Consciousness, part of the mind of God. Listen for truth. Truth is truth wherever you hear it.

There is a vast energy force coming in now that will greatly affect the neck and throat. Indeed, if you are a sensitive, you will see light shining out of the back of the neck. Go with the flow of life, for no one can truly conceive how great this transition is. None can have access to all information, even at the end of this period. With regard to these transmissions, these are for general consumption. They are truths, to give you courage and to give you hope, joy of life and experience. As the last breath of the outworking of karma draws to a close, you will understand the experiences that you have all encountered. You will have knowledge of the experience that every living soul has had. You will not have access to all the knowledge of the cosmic forces, but you will have knowledge of all that has existed on this planet.

IX. THE PATHMAKERS

There is a job to be done, for now is the time of cleansing. The old must be burnt away in order for new growth to be made possible. This is dangerous, but necessary.

Consider the following three aspects of this change. There is the normal cycle of your own planet, with a new revolution about to begin. There is, corresponding with this, another cycle of the wheel of change also about to begin, one which relates to the outer atmosphere - the solar cycle. There is a third, the most important cycle, also beginning, the cosmic turning point. So you are now experiencing three energy shifts, each momentous in its own right, all occurring at the same time. The normal cycle of your planet has come full circle many times before, and in the past you have also experienced the completion of the outer solar cycle. But you have never before experienced the changes brought about by the revolving of the cosmic cycle. Indeed, at the last turning of the cosmic wheel, Earth did even not exist. This cycle cannot be measured in time. Again, we give you the analogy of a great cosmic breath. The duration of this great breath lasts from the first point of breathing in, to the last point of breathing out. Now the Cosmos is only a few moments away from the end point of the outbreath.

For most of you, your work is just beginning. Enough has been cleared for you to chart both your own pathway and that of others. We speak to those who can hear. A cleansing is now taking place. This is most evident with regard to the energies within individuals. These energies are now being raised, and are visible to those who are sensitive enough to see them, those who can see emanations from the body, as well as the etheric and astral body.

Individuals are being cleansed all the time. Clarity is needed at the beginning, the time is now, and there must be no hesitation. There can be none, for you are at a new beginning, and you are moving down the pathway with the new energy frequencies. When you start down this pathway, you may feel detached from those around you, even from those who are with you on this path. You are no longer part of the old Earth energy, you are part of the new order. The new order has been in the conscious mind of man for a very long time. It seeped in earlier this century. Indeed, much music and literature, many plays and films have been written, all of which encompass the ideals of the new order. But most of the writers, artists and musicians concerned received only part of the picture. Art is more stimulating when only half the revelation is shown, as this leaves the other half to the imagination of those who see and hear these works. Art has always been a catalyst for new thoughts, and never more so than in this century. Now art and music have fulfilled their purpose. The senses will align, and you will no longer need their stimulus. Music and art will transcend and transmute.

Never doubt that you are one with the universal Source. Although we speak of new energies and different frequencies, these are all part of the whole. They merely appear as new to you in your world.

70

Aggression, greed and negativity have now reached saturation point. You can see this clearly, and it is becoming visible to all. This enhanced vision has been highlighted by healers in the past. They asked for the truth of reality, and this was seen by all, because even in the midst of aggression and negativity, their crystal clarity could do its work. No longer is aggression hidden. It is now a stark reality, and you can see examples of it in every street, in every town. This is alarming for many, but in fact there is no more negativity than there was before, just that it is now being exposed in the light, being revealed, waiting to be cleared. The violence and aggression has come from underground, and has broken through from below the surface. This is related to the energy shift of the Earth that we have talked about before. The destructive forces are moving outwards, something which is much needed. Many of you have felt this in several different ways. In one sense the Earth is crying out, and in her tears she has released her darkness. There is violence in her tears, but how wonderful it is for her to clear and to cleanse, to be free at last.

Others will be able to see things with greater clarity, both mentally and intellectually, as well as on a perceptual level. This perception is shining through with diamond clarity, and is being seen by many. This is similar to your legend of the Pied Piper, for their energies are now leading the children away from trouble. The ones left behind are rich in greed and avarice, and they will mourn. But the children are pure, and they can hear the note of the Pied Piper calling, leading them to the garden that your Earth will become. It is for this reason we call you children of light, for within that light there is crystal clarity. The children of light are of many different ages, some are very old, others are young. The Pied Piper is a leader energy, leading them by sounding the notes of heightened frequencies. The children being led away may physically never reincarnate again. They have transcended the need for reincarnation, and yet they are still part of the whole.

This is not a time of torment and trauma, but a time of knowing, and of recognition of the diamond light of truth. In some ways this may seem harsh, for the light is either present, or it is not. There are no half measures. If the light is not present, it is no good your trying to create it, or trying to force an individual to see. It is as though they were blind. This is the stark truth. This has much to do with the magnetic force, for where there is no magnetism, people cannot be drawn towards it.

Within the new frequencies there is an affinity with those who have the higher notes. This does not mean that where the opportunity arises, you should not calm and love and be compassionate to those who do not have the notes. Indeed, you have an absolute responsibility to treat them well, but you cannot, in truth, help them forward.

Souls are rejoicing as they are finally being released from the astral plane. If you listen, you can hear their song. They are now joining the choirs of angels in the higher realms of the astral, for they have completed their journey - songs of light, notes of light rejoicing.

Cosmic changes of such enormity do not occur instantly in just a matter of minutes or days, however you will notice certain shift points. We can describe it thus: During a full eclipse of the sun, darkness descends as the moon gradually obscures the disc of the sun. Finally the light is completely blocked out. Then, within a short space of time, the light returns. There is a point when the sun becomes completely obscured by the moon. It is in this instant that man is aware of the constant ever moving wheels of the sun and the moon. And so it is that there are points in time, like during the eclipse, when the reality of movement and change hit the conscious mind, although they have been moving all the time.

The clouds are clearing now. The energy of the astral plane, with the last remnants of emotion, is being drawn away, and sometimes this generates a final emotional convulsion. As yet the astral has not completely cleared and will not do so for a while, but more and more of you are suddenly becoming aware of the clearing of the clouds. This is similar to that which we spoke about earlier. As the clearing takes place, so the path can be seen. This has only just become visible. The path is new, but gradually it is being revealed. At the clearing point of the emotions some will feel an emptiness. We speak gently and kindly now - you will sense an emptiness in some, an almost zombie-like quality. Others will become like an empty shell. The energy within these particular individuals is too dependent upon the emotions, so as the changes unfold, they will become disorientated and vacant. This is not evil or darkness, but rather the creation of a void. You cannot help those who do not have enough soul light. However, as like attracts like, you will come into contact with many whom you can help. You must be selective who you talk to about this. Only speak to those who will understand, or where some knowledge of this is deemed to be essential. The wisdom of the orb is important now. When people are clouded in negative energy they draw more negativity to themselves through their need to associate with it. At this time of cleansing, it is very damaging for you to take alcohol or drugs. If you could see the damage this causes to the psychic centres and to the etheric body you would not indulge in such things. Taking what you call mind expanding drugs is extremely dangerous. They can cause you to let in the dark astral energies which we spoke about earlier. Drugs do not expand the soul. Expansion of the mind is much easier without them.

There are many good souls who are not quite strong enough to jump the vortex. Some of these are electing to die at this time, some *en masse*. They are choosing this now because there are many light beings, both above and below, who are able to help them. By leaving the physical now they have a greater opportunity for growth. They clear very quickly once they are in light, and they send you thanks for the work that many of you have done in clearing the darkness.

Some of these souls, because of positive links and because of the knowledge they now have, will move up into the higher realms. They will gather together and help with the clearing of the astral plane. They are saluting you now because they are free. The soul can move on. So do not be alarmed by sudden deaths, for in many cases the beings who die are the more fortunate ones. Dear children, it is hard for you to accept the passing of people you know and care about, it is hard even when you have seen them suffering in pain. Remember, when a person dies they do so because their soul has chosen this. Physical death may be preferable for some souls because they are too weak to take the new frequencies. Rejoice in their passing, for they are passing into light.

Those of you who are pathmakers must take your responsibilities seriously. You must be selective about whom you give your energy to, and draw back when it is not possible for you to help. You will know. This is an exciting time for all, for the physical and the spiritual winds are now blowing. Imagine walking along a path. It is cloudy and the weather is stormy, so you hold your head low, protecting yourself from the wind and the cold. Suddenly the clouds dissolve into the heavens, and you feel warmth radiating from the sky. You hold your head up and lift your face to feel the heat of the sun. This is what you are doing now, you are walking into light. The new light brings a greater warmth to the globe, which is truly a profound reality. This process taking place now is unavoidable and beautiful, the end of an enormous cycle of cosmic changes.

Dear children of light, you are already travellers in time. You can be wherever and whenever you want to be. You have access to all you need. The giant Cosmos is divided into two parts. Each half has no knowledge of the other. But within your sphere you will know both, for during the changeover you will see the one you have come from and the one you are moving to. You are privileged, for you will see more from your new perspective than any single entity has ever seen before. This is part of the greater expansion. Every minute the Cosmos is expanding. The Cosmos is not a set size, shape or time. It is ever expanding, and is expanding in experience. You are already flying in time, and the knowledge of this is now permeating into your consciousness.

Long ago, information was programmed into certain crystals. These crystals are like an entity, a living computer. It will not be long, however, before they disintegrate. This will occur once you have absorbed the knowledge that is stored within them. After that they will physically no longer be needed, for by then their energy will have been transmitted and received. It is not necessary for you to know where these crystals are located in physical terms, although you probably already know, but choose not to remember. This is not important. What is important is that you absorb the information contained within them. Some of you have already completed this process.

We leave you today with an image of yourself in a boat sailing over the horizon. You know you are safe inside the boat, but as it moves over the horizon, it disappears out of the view of those left behind. Many cannot see the pathmakers, but this does not matter, for the heightened energies are present, leading you all towards the mountains of another world.

X. THE FINAL CLEANSING

Your planet is at a turning point of the Cosmos. This shift point is moving you on to a new reality. The consciousness of man is awakening, which is a great leap for mankind, similar in scale to that when life emerged from the sea, when life became able to survive in air. You are mutating to a point where you can breathe the air of cosmic consciousness.

Your last world war was, in some ways, the war to end all wars, for there was a consensus decision made by the consciousness of man to take the light path at all costs. At that point, once the decision had been taken, evil days became numbered. Evil has had to worm its way up to the surface in order for it to be dissolved. Soon, many of you will pierce the veil. We have spoken much about fear and negativity. We will now leave this subject, saying only this: the final leap into a state of pure consciousness can only be taken when fear is completely eradicated.

You are now stargazers, dear children of light, for you have opened the gate into cosmic consciousness. This will have an enormous impact upon you, for greater knowledge is now accessible to you. Knowledge has always been obtained through knowing and accepting a greater reality. This explains how man was able to invent flying machines, for the spark of knowing that flying machines were possible, allowed them to be so. You now have a spark of realisation that you are part of the whole

Cosmos, that you exist and you live in that reality. Knowing you are participating in the reality of the Cosmos means you can journey to the stars, both in a physical and a metaphysical sense. You could never make this journey without the knowledge that you *can* travel to the stars.

We speak to you of love. Most of you understood love to be the sum total of all the positive energy on your planet, and accepted this also had a counterbalance of hate and negativity. This meant the plane of your experience was a balance on a scale between positive and negative. This is what makes your planet karmic - cause and effect, male and female, positive and negative. Your scientists believe all planets work in this way, but they do not. Indeed, your type of planet is rare in the Cosmos. Now all the love, the sum total of all that is positive, is moving on. This cannot be destroyed, but it is moving upwards. Your planet is now moving beyond the state of positive and negative. You will have pure energy, light force energy, a light without a shadow. The love will be drawn up into the higher light force, where it will excel, leaping into the light force. Negativity will dissipate and dissolve. Much of what we are saying is about this clearing. And for the next few years there will be a cleansing tide washing over your planet, from the smallest grain of sand to the most exalted being. The Cosmos is vast, dear children, worlds are being born and dying all the time; there is constant change.

You talk about stability. Your planet is ever turning, ever moving, ever changing. Is that stability? There is always a constant rhythm of change. Take your thoughts beyond your planet for a moment. Look at it. It is turning. See how it moves around your sun within your solar system. Further out you can see your solar system is also moving, part of the great cosmic chain. Your solar system is now moving into the vortex of new energies. Energy is coming into your solar system as pulses of energy, pulses which are becoming stronger. Some of you are aware of this. These pulses of energy will increase even more over the next two or three years; then, having drawn in greater and greater energy, Earth will begin to acclimatise herself to these new energies, and will no longer be so restless.

These pulses of energy, which are passing through your solar system, are transparent in nature, but where they impinge upon planets and other energies, they meet with some resistance. You will become increasingly aware of these impulses. They are becoming much stronger. These are affecting everything that exists on your planet, affecting everything that you can see, not just living things, but also metals, stones and other inanimate objects. Chemists will have difficulty with their reactions as bonding will be affected. Particles and molecules will not behave as they should, and this will cause some accidents, for the chemical bonding of materials will become more difficult. In a few instances the opposite will occur. Materials that should not react will instead react and bond. Mainly, however, the influence of the new energies will bring about a deterioration of the bonding of molecules within metals and other substances. The molecules in your bodies are also changing, transmuting in light.

In many ways there is not a lot more we can suggest you do. Keep calm, keep others calm, and cultivate a stillness within. The tide is turning and cannot be stopped. Better to ride the giant waves of change, for to resist is to destroy yourself. Those who are able to pull themselves out of the negative waters and breathe the air of the Cosmos, can move forward and work with the new energy. Others may not. Dispensing with negativity will allow the positive magnetic force of the soul to move upward.

We speak to you now of cosmic energies, those beings which exist outside the realm of your world. We are talking of different energies - light force beings, very different from you, some which you cannot yet see with your human eyes. Some of you will be able to see them, and they will appear to you as translucent beings, like a cloud.

You know there are sounds which you cannot hear, sounds which have a frequency above that of your threshold of hearing. The same is true of light, for you cannot see those beings that are above your threshold of sight. Their touch is so unfamiliar, you would not realise it if you touched them. When they come close, you may feel the faintest of sensations, or perhaps even nothing at all. Some beings are more visible than others. You talk of beings coming in from other planets, but many do not have a home in the sense that you understand this. They are fluid and, in your terms, they travel throughout the Cosmos without the need of vehicles to transport them.

Your planet has not been interfered with to any great extent, although from time to time a new genus of energy has been impregnated into your peoples. But for the most part your planet is a sanctuary, off limits to beings from elsewhere. In any case your reality is so different from theirs, they have nothing to offer you, and there is nothing they could take from you. Your green planet was left alone to work through its own karmic destiny. This has been respected by the cosmic energies. However, now that the changes have begun, they are being allowed in.

They are very curious about you, especially now that you have acknowledged them on some level. En masse you became consciously aware of their existence about forty years ago when two things occurred. First, man realised it was possible physically to leave his own atmosphere, and second they sensed the changes which you are experiencing. They are curious, like birds watching from a perch in a tree. It is true that some tried to interfere in a negative way, but very soon they realised they were not permitted to do this, and so they left. Remember, while you are in your physical body, it is not possible for you to see everything. There are many things that are beyond your range of experience.

We speak again of the co-operation of energies. The smallest breaths in the Universe are perfecting the Cosmos at both ends of the scale. You are all together. Your planet was, in one sense, removed, for it once stood at the edge of the Cosmos, where unrivalled in its sensations, it shone like a star. Where your planet has been, others will now take its place. There is a season for everything, and still man has not yet reached his full potential. There are no limits, only those which you impose upon yourselves. We have added some sweeteners to this information, for had we spoken too bluntly, even those who have made the leap might not have listened. For these messages have also been given to others in absolute terms, but they did not listen. We say nothing to promote fear, and we give you only the truth. So let us stand, hand in hand, as together we take the great Cosmic breath.

The sound of the universal trumpet is calling. Listen to the drums beating out a rhythm of cosmic information. The sound of the drums beating is pulsing energy, stimulating and transmuting your world. This energy is coming in like a cosmic wind, blowing and vibrating, an energy of pure light. Although we have had some difficulty in describing this energy, we call it light. One cell interacts with another, but when a third appears there is a fight, because only one is able to interact with the third. The first cell must then move on. The new energy is like the third cell. This is like a new sun, a new source of energy. So your planet will survive, and will make the interaction, but it will turn and shift to accommodate the new bonding of cells in universal terms. As your planet turns, it emerges into the starkness of light. Bright light. Clearer than the clearest day.

From behind your nose, you can hum. Feeling the stimulation, just behind your nose. You can "see" through this centre if you so choose.

As the energy moves, your own sun's rays will affect you differently. Be careful, the sun's rays are more potent now. Some of you will not be able to tolerate the action of the sun shining on your skin. There are still some things that you are not yet ready to hear but, we assure you, everything that is happening is happening as it should.

XI. THE COSMIC BREATH

There is a level of understanding at which there is no need for words, no need for communication in the normal way. This is a way of being beyond the level of personality. It is impossible to explain this to those who have had no experience of it, but we speak of it now as some of you will soon be experiencing it. Some of you will *know*. It happens when layer upon layer has been unfolded, uncloaking the soul, dissolving the remnants of the astral, of the individual. The individual can then link directly, without interference from the astral clouds.

There comes at this point what you could perhaps define as the conscious connection. This is neither the end nor the beginning, it is part of the great plan. When we speak of the great plan, we are not talking of a plan mapped out in advance like a jigsaw puzzle, we are talking of the knowing consciousness, beingness - the great breath. Within that great breath, all and everything is possible. All experience, all expansion, all mutation is largely a matter of choice. And when this returns to consciousness, it brings details of the experience back into the whole, ready to breathe out again, with the next cosmic breath.

This is much too great to describe in a way that the human mind can comprehend. The human mind is opening to many other facets now, to many other sights and sounds. But even at the very limits of its working, you could never fully understand. The only means of understanding is through the unlocking of the soul mind, which only occurs when the individual's soul has reached a point of consciousness. Your soul has a mind, and the capacity of the soul mind is far beyond that of your human mind. In one sense, the duality and polarity between the soul mind and human mind does not occur in other beings of other worlds.

There are still some of you, even those who have awakened, who find it difficult to conceive of a time when there will no longer be this polarity on your Earth. You will see for yourselves a beautiful orb existing solely in light, only in consciousness, without darkness, polarity, or karma.

The cosmic breath is gentle. It is absolutely gentle, but firm, and nothing can resist it. The great breath is like a hurricane wind with an energy of cosmic proportions. Yet it still has the gentleness of a baby's breath.

There is no shoulder to cry on, for you must follow your own paths of light. In the end you have to do this on your own. However, the all-encompassing breath, the all-encompassing love is there for all. Hold fast! By the time these words are put in print, there will be a real need for the world to hold fast. Do not get embedded in your sympathy, cut through it like a steel sword. Some people may think you are being hard, but this will not be so. You are just being strong.

All places of worship and any place that is used as a spiritual home must now realise that they are not all powerful. Theirs has been a way, a path, but you are now seeing signs of religions breaking up, for they hold too fast to their concept of being the only way, the only truth. We say to you all: there is no one path nor a single spiritual home that holds the only truth. *Your soul is the ultimate place of worship.* Truth is free, it is available to all if you honestly abandon your desires and ambitions, and do not make excuses. There are, indeed, places of sanctuary. But these can only be as swing doors to another reality. And some walk in and then out again, experiencing no difference. Accept, dear children, accept. Everything is as it should be; children are singing a new song of life.

If you could see with perceptive vision the colours of the aura of your world at this point, the predominant colour would be yellow. This is because the emotional energies are rising up to the surface, like curds of milk. They will be drawn upwards and then they will dissipate. They are coming to the surface. This, of course, includes emotions such as fear, anger and distress. If people were to lose their emotions too suddenly, this would kill them, because emotional energy has been such a power source for so long. They would, however, die in purity, as much of the darkness is emotional.

Above the yellow is another energy, one which you are not yet familiar with, one which we can describe as an energy of soft pink. This is acting like the clouds that draw up the rain. This energy has only just arrived, for it can only now be present, as a result of the work that has been done on clearing the negative astral. There is now, in one sense, space for it to exist. The soft pink cloud is rising up from the surface of the Earth, and also from individuals. This is having an enormous effect upon the animal kingdom. Some animals will suddenly die, but do not be alarmed by this. You will hear about instances of whole groups of people or animals suddenly dying in very strange circumstances. Many people will say this is a manifestation of evil. But this is not be the case, indeed, you could say it is quite the opposite. Negativity and evil are being cleared from living beings, which will cause the mass deaths of some. This new ray is entering your globe. It is moving, not fixed, and it is becoming stronger. It has just begun to permeate the astral darkness, through the space you have cleared. This can most certainly be called a ray of hope. Along with this mellow pink energy there are angel beings, gently guiding. At least four new rays will come in, prisms of light, octaves of sound.

Within the Universe there is a co-operation taking place on an instinctive level. Most of this is happening without your being consciously aware of it. Often, it is better not to be conscious of it, because the conscious mind can get in the way of right action and thought. Those of you who have jumped the vortex, and have melted into the light with the Source, have the desire to co-operate in this way. Trust. Trust that all is well, for all is right, all is for the best.

We will attempt to paint you a picture which expresses the beauty of the change. This will not be adequate but it may suffice. Imagine a windy day, with clouds moving swiftly across the sky, continuously changing shape, all moving together, one layer upon another. This is how it is, the universal movement, layer upon layer, creating new shapes all the time. When we speak of colours, we are not speaking literally, of real colours or real sounds, but of energy and connections. And yet some can understand this energy in terms of colours and sound, as a cosmic song in the Universe and a cosmic dance. Some of you will understand how this works in all its bounty, working in unity. No distraction. There is only expansion and growth.

Where there is darkness your light will shine forth. This you understand, so shine your light. Do not get involved with darkness. Be calm, shine, and radiate, for this will allow those who *can* be helped to be helped. To some you will appear to be insensitive, or perhaps unfeeling. Follow your intuition, for you know what you must do and when you must do it.

Some of you are despairing of the pollution on your planet. Some of this pollution is a result of the clearing we speak of, part of the darkness emerging from below the surface. The Earth is moving, shifting. By releasing some of its content in the form of volcanic eruptions, she can ease the pressure. Where there are releases of oil, this also assists the process. We spoke of the analogy of curds of milk floating to the surface. This is a good description. Much that is below the Earth will have to come to the surface, to release and make space for the new. We know you want to assist, but so many times we have said to you, the greatest assistance you can possibly give is to consciously and co-operatively radiate your individual light. You do not have to direct it to any specific place, for it will be drawn where ever it is needed.

Think again of the image of the clouds on a windy day. Imagine the energy being blown to where it is needed most. Again, we speak of the silent co-operation. It is so important for those who find their still light, their rock-like strength, to be aware of it, and to know that it works. When you concentrate your prayers on parliament or on people of power, you are confused about what is important in this world. Parliamentary buildings and the people inside them are not important in cosmic terms. They have no effect as a body on the changes we speak of. They are important only for the personality and the karmic working out of the individuals concerned. They have no importance with regard to the greater consciousness.

People in these positions are busying themselves with what they do largely for their own self-interest. There are a few people with higher consciousnesses who have attained office in these places. These people affect the higher energies through their radiance, although they may have lowly positions, perhaps in an office or a post room, so they are not recognised by the outside world. So send out your thoughts to spread the light and the energy and the consciousness to where ever it is needed, not to one particular place. This shall be done.

On a higher level, the consciousness will be blown where it is needed for good. There is no going back and no indecision. Governments have only human power. They do not have the power of the consciousness, the higher power of the consciousness which leads them. On a cosmic level, politicians are not powerful. But as all energy moves as one, on some level they have their minor part to play. They are but pawns in the eternal movement of light. Your planet has moved beyond the danger point where evil could have won. There is no chance of it taking over now.

The higher the energy of an individual, the more it

expands, until it reaches a point of unison with other higher energies. At this point you could say you become less individual, as you are then working in unison with others. But you are still an individual who, for whatever reason, has to live out his or her own earthly life span. The soul mind is inside, working in unison with others. The soul is timeless and, as such, it is a time traveller. On your physical level, you are ruled by time, but on a soul level, you are not. And those who reach the higher consciousness level will experience a feeling of timelessness. This is part of the reason why you feel detached from your fellow man, and from your planet. You become as one time, one place. But within that one time, that one place, all and everything and all is happening as it should.

There will come a point, after the major transition taking place on the planet, where several higher consciousnesses will travel in time. The energy of the consciousness may move into another body, or it may keep its own body, depending on what is required. It may travel to the outer realms of the Universe, or it may stay where it is. When you reach that level there are no barriers in time or space.

The higher consciousnesses that are here are more numerous than usual. They are needed now. They are part of the great breath, part of the expanding Universe. Light and light forces. They come from the past and from the future, to help in this, the most important time in your planet's history.

The akashic records can be described as the books in which all the experiences of your planet are recorded. There is a similar, but not identical, computer-like information source or consciousness, which contains information regarding everything in the Cosmos. The akashic records will very soon be absorbed into this consciousness. So, to put it simply, if you want to find some information, you will have to look in a different library.

To future teachers we say: you do not need to do anything, *just be.* Answer the questions put to you. Calm and heal all those who come to you, and know that by your magnetism you will draw people to you who can be helped. The emanations of the higher consciousness send light wherever it is needed. This may be directed to your buildings of power, or it may be sent to aid in the control of pollution, or to help the starving masses. Keep up your meditations and prayers. You will automatically know whether you have to move or stay where you are.

With some species of animals there has been a grouping of souls. This is very beautiful to watch. What this means is that some are be able to act as healers for their species.

Every last piece of negativity is being brought to the surface now. You can see this, even in the births of children. And should there be mass deaths in unusual situations, do not be alarmed, for most likely their soul energies had already departed before they died. Energies come in waves. All consciousnesses on this planet are helping in the final transmutation of the dark forces. Know that. Know you are all part of the great Cosmic dance.

XII. NEW BIRTH

You are discovering your own divinity, your own connection to the Source. This is a very positive time for your world. Never before have there been so many light forces on your planet, both above and below, all working towards the greater good, the greater light.

We have spoken much in these sessions about energies and magnetism. We have endeavoured to give you a picture of how they correlate and correspond, not just within your own planetary field of existence, but within the Cosmos as a whole.

As parents you watch your children grow. You delight in their growth. We speak of our delight in you, because it is clear that you are entering a new stage of growth and existence. This is not the end. It is illuminating. With all energies working together, within your soul, understanding can be complete.

You are experiencing the fruits of your endeavours through the aeons of time, through all the experiences that you have had. And yet time is one. Joyousness rises up and lifts all with it.

Some of you have now come to a point where you no longer have the need to know. Having reached a point of beingness and rounded consciousness, you find living within the confines of your Earth somewhat restricting. But you recognise that this is something that has to be done. You are on Earth because your consciousness raises those of others around you. In reality, when you come to this point of being, you need not remain in your human body. But, at this special time, your consciousness elects to stay in your body for the sake of the work that you can do for humanity as a whole.

We have spoken much about the dissipation of the emotional body. This is important, but it is not over yet. There is still much to do. If you roll a stone down a hill, the further it travels, the faster it moves. In a sense, you planet is like a rolling stone which is now approaching the bottom of the hill, and is accelerating faster and faster. So much is happening for you in such a short space of time. Again we say, you are experiencing the last moments of the great outbreath. Time will appear to speed up even more over the next few years, before a point of balance is reached once again.

When a baby is born it immediately takes its first independent breath into its lungs. These lungs, up to the point of birth, have grown strong within the mothers womb, ready for use. Like the baby's lungs, the new energy centres are now growing at a rapid pace. Your planet, your humanity is reaching the point when the new energy centres will be ready, when, at it were, it will be time for birth. These centres will then breathe in the new forces. And just as when a baby is born it lets out a yell to acknowledge new life, humanity will let out an enormous yell when it opens its "lungs" to the new forces.

Some of you are already opening these new energy points within your skull, but the mass of humanity will do this together in one great breath as a counterpart to the great shout. This note will resound throughout the Universe, and will join with other sound frequencies to create new life. This shout or yell is an expression of joy, as any midwife who has heard that yell will tell. How we wait to hear that yell, telling us of the new creation. The time for this is coming very soon now.

All of you will have to find your point of being, not doing. You will do without plans - knowing, trusting, willing as situations arise. Those who have begun to take in the new breath will be in the right place at the right time. There cannot be any doubt, for it is impossible for you not to be where you should be, such is the strength and magnetism of the consciousness.

Nothing can go wrong now. Your planet is set on its course. We say this specifically to those of you who are looking outside for answers, and seeing the trouble that the mass of humanity is in, say this is wrong. Listen, lest you become oppressed by this, and get sucked into humanity's fears. Your planet has passed beyond the moment of choice. It has chosen a right path, and is moving forward to the birth, to the growth of new forces. These are new to your planet, but not to the Cosmos.

For some time now, male and female energies have become interrelated, less clearly defined. You have seen this on the lowest levels and on the highest. Those of you who know about the union with God know that there is a point where the male and female within the individual become as one. In humanity's terms, the changeover will be noticeable, in that both male and female energies are becoming as one.

This is happening on a large scale, with male and female, positive and negative becoming less clearly defined. This is one of the reasons why you have had fluxes of energy passing through your planet. These are particularly affecting the use of electricity, for as the negativity becomes earthed, positive and negative are quite literally altering.

This will stabilise, but you will notice that in some places the electrical forces will be stronger. The male and female energies of your planet are coming together. And when they do there will be new birth, new growth, new being. Your planet is coming into new being - the birth, the creation of the new force. Your planet is mutable and very strong. In cosmic terms the changes taking place are extremely small. Viewed from the outside you might assume they are almost insignificant - a tiny globe in a tiny system in the corner of the Universe. However, the effects of its energy have been felt by many forces for many long years. Earth is now metamorphosing into a leader energy of universal proportions, and will cease to be the insignificant planet it is now, coming to its rightful place as a leader. Every energy inter-relates with every other energy. Every world, every particle, every speck of dust is an important part of the whole.

Sometimes during the great cosmic breath, a particular energy force or world takes on the qualities of a leader - a great magnetic force of universal proportions, helping and inspiring other globes and other beings. Earth is, quite literally, becoming magnetic, and when you think on this, you realise how people and the life forces on your planet need to change, have to change, are changing - changing positively.

We have learnt so much from you, and we thank you for this. We have learnt so much from your experiences, from your ordeals and from your joys. Through the experiences you have given us, we can take this new breath with greater strength, vigour and positive light. As the new breath comes into being, we have no way of knowing what effect this will have, because once again we are at a starting point for the Cosmos. Energy is free, and we do not have information about what will happen to beings, planets and forces. What we can say is the experiences of renewed energy, light forces and growth, in which your planet has played an important part, have given the whole Cosmos new life, new power and new light.

So, as a the child takes in the breath of the great cosmic change, it will let out a yell and release the power once again, setting free the light forces for further experience, greater joys, greater love and greater energy.

Know the part you have played in the great cosmic dance, and know that you are privileged to be part of the birth of the new cosmic breath.

Titles by Julie Soskin from Barton House Publishing:

The Wind of Change
The Cosmic Dance

Recently, Julie channelled the information that there will be a third book in this series...

For advance notice of forthcoming new titles please write to us and request to be put on our mailing list. We will also keep you informed of workshops led by Julie Soskin.

A WORD FROM THE PUBLISHERS...

Our aim is to bring the works of Julie Soskin and the other authors we publish to the widest possible audience. Please can you help us with this:

If there are any book shops which you feel ought to be stocking our titles, but currently do not, please let us know. We are also interested in contacting booksellers and individuals, who live outside the UK, who wish to distribute or sell our titles abroad.

Many people have called or written to us requesting several copies of this book, either for re-sale, or for presentation as gifts to friends. We are delighted to supply these on the following preferential terms:

Five copies or more of The Cosmic Dance *UK p&p free.* (overseas orders only *add £1.50 per book* airmail)

Order ten copies and get *two additional copies free, UK p&p free.* (overseas *add £1.50 per book despatched* airmail)

NB. Single copies are £5.99 plus £1.50 p&p per book. (overseas add £3.00 per book airmail, total £8.99 sterling).

Please make cheques payable to *'Barton House Publishing'*
9 Barton Orchard, Bradford-on-Avon, BA15 1LU, UK. Call 02216 7705.
Access, Visa, Mastercard, Eurocard welcome, state number and expiry date.